Ten Dimensions

of

Philosophy and

Religion in the

Digital Internet Age

Georg E. Schäfer

For Leon and Paul and the younger generation

About this book:

How influenced the Information and Communication Technology -ICT- from the 1960s till now our awareness of philosophy and religion? The development of ICT was fast and disruptive in generation steps of three to five years. Since the development of the Internet, later the Search Engines bringing all knowledge of the world to our finger-tips, and now the social networks with excellent speech recognition in many fields of applications, we feel that our mind was surprised by this development. Our mind didn't follow these technology generations in a transparent way. The technology is difficult to understand. Irritation and undiscovered consciousness are within our souls and hearts. Now we urgently need orientation. Nobody described in a general and easy to understand overview what to expect now from philosophy and religion. Many of our beliefs are contradictory but conflicts are not transparent. This book shows and documents where our mind lost sight of important changes. Future challenges are described. Easy to understand help to solve everyday problems is provided. This is a framework for our personal ethics and thinking.

About the Autor Georg E. Schäfer:

Georg E. Schäfer studied Mathematics, Physics and Computer Science. He worked in the Information and Communication Technology (ICT) Industry as Development, Project and Sales Engineer. Later, in the Ministry of Interior in Baden-Württemberg, he served as front-runner of state ICT, responsible for co-ordination of state ICT with the ICT of the federal government and the local government and for the implementation of the latest technology in state administrations. For ten years he represented the German Bundestag in a High-Level Committee of the European Commission. Georg E. Schäfer is now retired and in the board of a church committee. All his life, he was interested in philosophy and theology. Now he has the time to add to his ongoing studies on the development of ICT (like Quantum Computers and Artificial Intelligence with Neural Networks and Algorithms) the fascinating world of philosophy and theology as a main field of interest.

Bibliographic Information of the German National Library: This publication is registered and detailed information is available in the Internet on dnb.dnb.de.
© 2018 Georg E. Schäfer
Printed and Published by: BoD – Books on Demand, Norderstedt
ISBN: 9783752887891

Bibliografische Information der Deutschen Nationalbibliothek: Die Deutsche Nationalbibliothek verzeichnet diese Publikation in der Deutschen Nationalbibliografie; detaillierte bibliografische Daten sind im Internet über dnb.dnb.de abrufbar.
© 2018 Georg E. Schäfer
Herstellung und Verlag: BoD – Books on Demand, Norderstedt
ISBN: 9783752887891

Content

Your Philosophy can Glue the Satanic Split

In moments when we need orientation, we feel the gap between our daily life and our incomplete awareness of its foundations. Emotionally and mentally, we live in the past, but we use rather competent the new tools of the digital Internet age we got in the last few years. Most of us failed to update and harmonize the understanding of our situation, of outdated beliefs still active and the ethics now appropriate. This can hurt. Especially as hardly anybody offers an integral orientation. The complexity of our world and the difficulties to understand the latest technology prevents professional philosophers and theologians from drawing a complete theory. Strictly based on arguments and with modesty, we give ten main pillars, called ten dimensions. This offers valuable orientation and advice.

Haughty people tell proudly that they believe nothing. When they finally explain their attitude, they tell a long list of beliefs. Fact is, we have no alternative to a life based on beliefs. But we are left alone. For more than a hundred years, philosophers didn't draft a complete philosophy covering the most important aspects of our life. Theologians preach beliefs, we cannot share anymore. And both use an arrogant language only full-time experts can understand. We want to do that better.

In this book, we introduce the concept of myths to better understand belief, mental attitudes, soul and heart concerns. The world is full of myths and we don't realize the impact. The same way we train to use an online search engine, we must train philosophy and religion. Here is a direct and thrilling entry point into the thinking of the best and the brightest modern trends. We go there directly without detours.

Our world changed with the Internet and the digital services like Messengers, Artificial Intelligence, Neural Networks and things like Bitcoin and Quantum Computers. These are not all issues of (the public) Internet, so we call our current knowledge-based world a "**digital Internet age**". Most of us are not aware of the mental changes we made in the last twenty years or since World War II. Here we create this awareness.

Let's face it. Some need to think about religion and philosophy daily. Others deal with these subjects from event to event and from time to time. Here we give an overview for all. The reader can start anywhere in the book and lay it aside when the thirst is satisfied.

The Satanic Split

Fifty years ago, people lived in a homogenous world. A clear majority appreciated the same music, heard the same news and most parents believed in the same education objectives. These are just a few examples of a once homogenous world. Today, we live in another world. It is split into heterogenous groups, people are more lonesome, and too many people search their identity. Imagine e.g., you believe in organic food and you want to live in a sustainable way to save the planet. Then you own a payback card for green shops. In the social network, you support politicians and lobby groups for a green policy. Very soon, about seventy to ninety percent of your information input comes from green groups and their environment. This is due to the digital Internet and its procedure, implemented everywhere, to deliver opinions you already shared! Your digital activities will be recorded by the search engines, the cookies on your device and back your arguments. After some years you might be fundamentally convinced of all green activities. This is not bad. Bad is the technology that unconsciously narrows your thinking.

Imagine, you follow religious groups, attend Christian services in your community and you meet families with the same basic Christian attitude. Then you register in religious, Christian, Internet groups and your information input is mostly from this side. The Christian groups might split up, in one group that believes in the holy word of the bible, without any interpretation, and in another that is more liberal. You will make your choice. In the next years, you will receive mostly information from the group you chose. Unconsciously, you begin to see the other groups as adversaries.

These examples show how our society currently breaks apart in different groups and how these groups become more radical by time. This is the split we are talking about. It is a split caused and accelerated by the digital Internet.

There is no doubt that this split is killing our society and our cultural identity. It may start wars, some say. We must avoid this split. This split is satanic because if it continues we risk building the basis of World War 3. From history we know that in the year 1913 suddenly World War 1 started, in a world everybody supposed to be secure and open-minded and economically dependent. It started like a game of politicians, cheered by the crowds, and ended after millions of dead people, then depressed by years of cruel war. This cannot be the perspective for our children.

Christian beliefs and theology cannot glue the people together. Because the religious groups are split, too, and unable to unify their believers. Religious groups take their beliefs from dogmas. Philosophy can glue this split because a philosopher does not write down dogmas but axioms. These are open and can be changed by everyone and whenever someone feels that other axioms are more suitable for the explanation of his or her life. We can build our own philosophy that way. With axioms philosophers build models, not some mental pressure called "the eternal truth". Philosophy does not have the concept of sin, punishment by God and loss of your soul, if you don't believe in a basic religious concept.

So, whatever religion we take, all of them cannot glue this terrible split of our society. It's only philosophy that can do it because philosophy is open-minded, ready to drop or extend axioms any time.

This is not astonishing as e.g. Christian theology did not yet accept the basic human rights of all people like equality of all people and freedom for everyone, the right to live (or to die if we are very sick), the right to pursuit our happiness, etc.

Philosophy does so. The constitutions of all democracies do alike.

To define our life and set up our personality, we create our own philosophy. Nobody else can do the job for us. Without such definitions, we drift in the wind of our various daily emotions. A balanced lifestyle, built on a good foundation, demands a personal philosophy. Without such a foundation, we cannot hold jobs with higher responsibility (like member of a board of directors or politician). Team members and citizen would otherwise have no confidence in our problem-solving capabilities and we would fail.

Philosophy and Religion for our Life

Despite the tremendous changes we undergo in the digital Internet age, many of us think that religion and philosophy are invariant over times and centuries. Being the holy revelation of our ethics and foundations of this world, shouldn't these messages last forever? The words of the Bible and the philosophers like Aristotle didn't change. We still read them in the original language or version. How can someone think that the interpretation of these holy scripts could change? These texts are true, aren't they the truth?[1]

Let us research these texts and submit our question about invariant validity to the original texts. We meet e.g. Paulus (named Saulus in Hebrew). In the meeting of the apostles in the year 48 A.D., he advocated the concept (revolutionary at the time) that persons can become Christians without becoming Jews before. He was successful. His initiative changed our religious world completely. Paulus' concept was not self-

---

[1] "True" and "false" are attributes of all possible statements. If something is true, someone must prove it. If there is no proof, the statement is not considered to be "true". Some people say that their religious beliefs are true, because they feel it, or know it somehow. This is not enough to qualify a statement as "true". "I know, Jesus speaks to me when I am in danger." may be considered "true" by the person who says so. We don't accept this "true" as it cannot be proved.

evident, as it opened a new paradigm to Christianity, the Hellenistic co-foundation of Christianity. Paulus stressed also the fact, that a new time began with Jesus. This proves that Paulus changed the interpretation of biblical texts twice. He taught that the historic books of the Bible had to be re-read with the spirit of Jesus. And in 48 A.D., he integrated Christianity and Hellenistic Philosophy.

Fact is, from the beginning of Christianity, a philosophical touch became part of this religion. During history till today this never ended but multiplied. Many more philosophical ideas were integrated into Christian beliefs. E.g. Martin Luther translated the Bible in the language of common people to allow all of us to interpret the text to the specific demands of our life. There is no end to the further interpretation of the Bible. Here we talk about the convergence of Christian religion and philosophy under the challenge of the digital Internet age. Generalized, we can now state the convergence of any enlightened religion with modern philosophy.

That cannot be true, one might say, thinking of religious dogmas like Christ's resurrection. There is no resurrection in any of the philosophies if we do not mix philosophy with religion and believe in a supernatural event. May be, we have some reserves on doctrines and interpret them in a very worldly way. We don't have necessarily to think of a supernatural resurrection. Don't we have our daily resurrection in the morning after a good sleep, finding things that troubled us last night to comfort us in the morning, having found out that they lead us towards a new direction? Maybe the texts of the scripts and books are invariant[2] but our understanding of them changes and matures step by step. This is true for the life of everyone and for the society.

There are many stories in the Bible that demonstrate us the stepwise development of our understanding and our concepts of the world. In parallel, our abilities to manage our environment are developing, too. The Bible says, that man should dominate and rule the world. This requires learning, slow development of wisdom and experience. Ruling the world, the plants, the animals and the environment isn't possible in a spontaneous action. We start somehow, we then see – like God – what is good and what should become better, and we learn by doing. Every morning when we rise, we can find new wisdom and new knowledge.

Our subject here is the wisdom and knowledge of the digital Internet age. This is of course no book about the functions of the computer, artificial intelligence or neural networks. We don't learn the concept of quantum computers or how to program a new social network software.[3] Here we investigate our logic as well as our hearts and souls. What do we really think? What are our needs and plain or hidden sorrows? How can we feel at home in this new world? What are our challenges and our possible achievements? How to maintain peace of our souls, of our families, our

---

[2] … unless new translations are found because of new historical discoveries.

[3] Technology ist explained in Georg E. Schäfer, Digitalisierung braucht Verstrauen, 2018, BoD

nations and the contradictions that we see as threats?

Some of us might say that there is nothing new. Where do you see anything new? Let us go back some hundred years, to the times when the church thought that the stars run on crystal balls around the earth. Galileo Galilei was one of the scientists who contradicted this perception simply by offering a telescope to those who didn't see the truth without. Obviously, there was change. Later the philosophy of the Enlightenment brought even more change to our interpretation of philosophy and religion. World War 1 and 2, especially with the atomic bomb, brought us again radical change into our concepts of a merciful and gracious God. Today we understand what the Bible means when it says that we are to manage our world ourselves. We have the digital services and the Internet to help. Rapidity and quality of our actions improved immensely. After World War 2, we learned that God gave us the ability to maintain peace or to lose it in World War 3.

What man can do is not the responsibility of God. We can dig our garden without Gods help and we water the plants by our own understanding of draught. We can politically manage our world as well. We can pray to God, we can meditate and discover what could be the best solution. **Peace and wealth of the world are not falling from heaven given by a gracious God. It is our duty, and our brain must work to build political and administrative concepts of peace and general comfort for all people.** This we learnt in the digital Internet age looking e.g. back at World War 1 and 2 and evaluating with modern logic the fact that it's men who discover new medicine, find new materials, find new methods to produce food and must create a new energy basis for billions of people on this planet.

After World War 2[4], in the digital Internet age new evidence, new challenges and new chances were coming along with the computers and their algorithms. Does this change our concepts of philosophy and religion? And if, how?

When our ancestors managed our world with digging the garden, ploughing the fields and developing agriculture they used a new tool and a new method whenever they considered it a better solution. Today, in the digital Internet world and the knowledge society, **we must use a new idea, a new algorithm whenever these prove to be better than what we had used before**. Looking at our knowledge world, we find that there are new and better concepts every day or even every hour. The race of the development is fast. Somehow, we must cope with it. Somehow, we must make our peace with this incredible speed, depth of ideas and quality of services. And 10% is reserved for leisure.

---

[44] We recommend Georg E. Schäfer, History of Computer Science, BoD.

Digital Internet Changed our Life Completely

It's basics, we talk about here, as an elaborated presentation of the digital Internet world needs more than one book. But it opens our mind for the discussion of philosophy and religion in the digital Internet age.

Highlights of Digital Age Influence on Philosophy and Religion

What are the changes that the digital Internet brought us with importance to religion and Philosophy? **Here is a list of the major influence of the digital Internet to philosophy and religion:**

- **The satanic split is a huge change of our social interaction and a threat to the identity of our society as described above.**
- **We get transparency and knowledge about all religions, all philosophies, all sciences (in a popular and a scientific version).** Search engines and other tools like avatars bring the wisdom and knowledge of the whole world to our fingertips. Nobody can fool us anymore. **We smelled the thrill of transparency .**

- **We became transparent in a way that never existed before (Big Data, Privacy). We must fight to maintain our personality.**
- Martin Luther translated the Bible from Latin into the language for ordinary people. Everybody could make up his mind then. The power of the Pope was reduced, the self-determination of all people was enforced. **Many modern avatars translate free of charge every language into every other language. The consequences will be even heavier than those of Martin Luther's work.**
- **We get plenty of everything especially knowledge and a new definition of our life.**
- **We demand and need participation on all political decisions.** To reduce the satanic split and to protect our natural environment needs the co-operation and support of everyone.
- **We can overcome complexity. We can, and we know!**
- **We argue the whole day with the rules of formal logic. We don't accept any kind of belief or wording that we don't understand.**
- **Religion and philosophy can propose but not dictate. We know how to assess beliefs / myths.** We create our personal philosophy.
- **We can calculate the individual future where we had only anonymous statistics.** As an example, we use

nutrition rules. Some years ago, these rules were the same for all people. Now we find detailed individual recommendations for special groups like patients with leukemia, weak muscles, eye sickness. In parallel, we find detailed individual data on survival after a serious sickness.

Let us investigate some subjects in more detail.

Diversity Shapes today's World

Our awareness is substantially a consequence of the conditions of our life. There is our prosperity, the peace we enjoyed for more than fifty years and the continuing progress with industrial productivity and Information and Communication Technology. These three success factors are not self-evident. The younger generation knows that from hearsay only. So, young citizen think, medical and pharmaceutical progress is self-evident. Many consider elections as being unimportant, because politicians do anyway what the users of social networks think is best.

Now we feel irritations. We recognize that we spoilt our kids, we overdid our social help and we created cultural and regulatory overkill. This begins with speech. Politically correct speech is now considered by many citizens as the distant, artificial speech of academically educated (arrogant) people. Normal citizen neither get the help nor the in-depth consideration for improvements in their daily life. Politically correct language is no more seen as something to help but to neglect the needs of important groups of our nations. Feeling this way, far too many follow, what is now called misleadingly, popular politicians. Italy and the U.S.A. in 2017 and 2018 may serve as an example.

Another aspect is the fact that whenever citizens can vote (e.g. in Poland, in the UK for BREXIT), especially the younger people don't do it. Many think, that posting an idea or an attitude in a social network instead of going to the ballot box may decide the outcome of an election. This is of course wrong. After the election, they demonstrate for their ideas, suddenly totally disillusioned. Too late! People lost their perception of real life and entered in a virtual life of dreams and hopes that does not work as expected.

Third thing is the heterogeneity of our society. More than half the population of the world lives in cities and megacities with growing tendency. There we live in a heterogenous crowd of neighbors, door to door. These are e.g. the citizen who like cities, those who like wild nature and strictly cook their organic food daily, those who don't cook anymore and prefer junk food to cooking a simple egg, those who are happy to live without a car, those who enjoy leaving with their recreational vehicle the cities during the weekend exploring the wild mountains. Probably we never had such a diversity of opinions and life styles ever before.

Too many of us live in an unsynchronized world of conflicting dreams, hopes and realities. They find no way out. There is a task for philosophy.

Why? We really have all the knowledge of the world at our finger tips. Our daily used avatar[5] systems with (among other techniques) their cookie management, like the search engines of the Internet, support our individual preferences. We get more information about our food, our popular travel destinations, the books and the shows we prefer etc. than about alternatives. The cookies and the avatars keep our mind in a firm cage. Living in a shell of our preferences, cut off from the world of our neighbors, makes us belief that everybody is evidently like we are. This, of course, is an illusion.

Plenty of All

Fifty or a hundred years ago, most families put some money aside to buy an object (e.g. a bike, new furniture for the bedroom, a fridge) they wanted for years. They went to a library to find the answer to difficult questions (like the importance of the "gold standard", the recipe for "canard à l'orange", a sketch for building a bird feeder). Now

---

[5] Avatars are pieces of hardware and software which simplify our life by doing a complex task for us in a totally satisfactory way. Examples are the transfer of speech to written language by Android smartphones with the help of the Google servers, using a search engine understanding complex questions and answering these with well documented complete results, shopping in large data bases (like Ebay) including our preferences.

we submit our questions to a search engine and we get the information desired in no time at all on our screen. Comparably easy, we get food (e.g. fresh bread 24/7, games, books even instantly if we choose an e-book). The standard service, we expect today, is consequently immediate, with rich choice and an entertainment-like presentation. Most of us expect such service at low cost or no cost (e.g. administrational services of e-government), too.

This changed our perception of the world. The change is positive if we are aware of it. But a growing number of us lose control because e.g. they don't understand Artificial Intelligence. How many, we don't know. The boundaries of the different groups in our society are not yet found out. Let's look at the extreme.

In this group, people lost contact to the real world and they live in a virtual dream-like world. E.g. they don't see any more the effort and the pain needed to produce things. They don't value the education and the devotion of qualified skilled workers and subsequently they don't value their products. Our shops are flooded with cheap look-alike products and quality products are only offered in niches for people who know the secrets of the production. Many of these dreamers expect doctors to cure them instantly, clergymen to console them immediately and partners who act synchronously with what they have in mind. This doesn't work. Therefore, queer cures are downloaded from the Internet. Instead of adhering to one consistent religion, these people believe into a contradictory medley of exotic world views ("Weltanschauungen"), being unable to lead a systematic life with true friends and consistent child education frameworks. Instead of patiently fighting out different opinions with their partner, they start the next phase of their life with another partner. People lost in this chaotic thinking lose the thrill and the satisfaction of looking deeper in oneself and revise beliefs and manners.

This is true only for the people living in the happy nations with constant growth and peace. Many of the other people, like some in Africa, learn the advantage of the smartphone without broadband access but enjoy many small and useful features. And much too many people live in dictatorships or slave-like dependencies in misery and without hope. We should never forget these people. They cannot interpret the Bible in the way the happy people do. Talking about religion and philosophy in the Internet age requires talking about the people who live in happiness and those who live in misery. The whole scale from good to bad is important. We never know when war, misery and need meet us again. That may be in a dark corner of the happy world or in a world that broke to pieces.

Participation in Decision-Making

We mentioned the diversity of people living side by side in a virtual world supported by the digital Internet within the same city. The bigger a city, the more heterogeneous groups exist with different or even adverse concepts of life. Social research found one concern all groups place emphasis on. All people request to participate in political and administrational decision making. On a local level, people prefer interviews and Internet questionnaires focusing on a single project. Less wanted is voting a specialized party or interest group every legislative period. The reason is that these parties and groups seem to be not trustworthy. Especially parties lost trust by giving objective A priority in the election phase and accepting later, when in power, a totally different objective B. This behavior is common in today's political life. Anyway, it is not accepted or not understood by voters and therefore eroding our democracy.

Citizen and consumers want to participate in defining and running a service. As a consumer, we can participate by the way we spend our money. If a high percentage of consumers buys a car with driver assistance and don't spend their money on comfort features, they participate. We hold it to be self-evident that we can chose and influence in this way, since Ford offered more colors and shapes than a black Model T. In our shops are not only black shoes like some time ago in communist countries. Our whole life as consumers involves choice. This is our life style. We don't intend to change it.

The adverse situation is offered by the government. Government administrations are organized everywhere in the world for every concern according to the rule "in a specific region one and only one agency is responsible for this concern". Otherwise there would be conflicts between administrations. Fact is, there is no choice for the citizen.

What is even more difficult to understand is another fact, namely that life is rather complex and full of contradictory objectives. E.g. we request the right to relax in a nature reserve and enter it with a recreational vehicle to stay for a week. On the other hand, hundreds or thousands of such vehicles damage the nature past recovery. Often agencies and governments are in such a fix to impose one of two bad alternatives: Let the people go in the nature parks and damage them. Or don't let people in and fear their anger. It's evident, compromises are the only solution. But extremists on both sides of the scale of actions don't accept the decisions taken by the authorities.

Only one way seems to lead us a way out of this fix. We need mature personalities with their own solid philosophy. Also, we more research on the content that must be decided. And we need a better preparation and later presentation of the decisions taken by the authorities.

In short, the idea is applying Big Data and Open Government.

Data is the resource of our century. Big Data are the tools to analyze any amount of data, no matter how big, in Milliseconds. What statistics are they creating? Statistics is not the only important application. Big Data e.g. analyzes research data about cancer genes totaling billions of data records. The result is wanted to find personalized (individual) cures within the antigen-antibody complex e.g. for leukemia. Other examples are immediate flash-like feedbacks about the quality of medical therapies when a diagnosis is entered into the computer.

The analysis of Big Data breaks down to individual behavior of everyone in the scope of the data, even if the name of the individual is not known. As an example, take our shopping in the supermarket. From the content and structure of our purchase bill, the supermarkets can nearly identify the individual household. Security cameras follow all individuals in a train station or in a shopping mall without prior identification. The way people walk, wait and loiter, inspect displayed goods etc. reveals their motivation with satisfactory probability. Thief, terrorists and other criminals can be monitored.

To state a résumé, the fact is that incredible quantities of Big Data bases exist as property of different organizations, private and public. Nobody has an overview, and nobody can co-ordinate private and public actions and decision-making in any reasonable way. In addition, these big data bases contain the data of identifiable persons. According to the principles of Data Privacy the data belong to the citizen and consumers and not to the owners or operators of the data bases.

Where we used statistics in the past (e.g. 70% of cancer patients can be cured), in the digital Internet age we can calculate for every patient the ways to cure him. This is of course much better than an anonymous statistic. It helps the patient. We now have the computer power and the insight to do so. **In the future, statistics will be substituted by individual calculation of among other things therapeutic cure, financial wealth,**

housing, job careers and individual, professional development. This will improve our life in a giant progress. To understand it, we compare this improvement with the development of pain killing drugs and birth control pills. These two developments brought an end to the most painful situations of people in the medieval world. It changed the role of pastors radically. Once responsible not only for theology but also for psychology, medicine and politics, pastors today have a small responsibility, mostly of theoretical religion and personal communication. Now Artificial Intelligence systems of bankers help people with immense debts more than the good advice of a parson. The relief of the person indebted is fundamentally deeper, too.

If we created a regulation that gives the individuals access to their data and the decision-makers an access to the data bases, both concerns would be met. It may look complex, but we solved already much more complex problems. First, a registration of the data bases and their content would be necessary. That wouldn't restrict any company in any way. Second, a limited access should be allowed for third party decision-makers to the data bases they feel the need. The limitation would apply for a time limit (e.g. during the planning phase) and a content limit (e.g. only statistics, only identifiable data records of the neighbors in a 5-mile circle). Third, something like the European Union's privacy directive should be installed in all nations.

Open government is a technique to provide full transparency to the public on political decision-making in all areas without classified material.

There is much progress these days. It started with ranking of schools, hospitals etc. Now even the basic data records are offered in a standardized way to citizen. They can download the records and process them with their home computer and public domain (license free) software. Of course, nobody expects that citizen now re-calculate whatever authorities calculated already. But in case of personal involvement and interest, the citizen can do so.

Complexity is a double tricky subject. There is no religion or philosophy earnestly teaching a life without complexity. First, life is complex. No help. Second, complexity is a means of establishing power. Governments, companies and churches often make regulations bureaucratic and complex to prevent citizen and parliament to interfere in what they want. This is a bad game and not acceptable. Fact is, we need full transparency and participation of all citizen when political decisions are needed. The Swiss do so successfully for hundreds of years.

Philosophy and Religion Converge

An audacious headline? We don't think so and offer some arguments. Convergence is based on the growth of formal science. In history, subjects unchallenged by formal science were left for religious and philosophical dispute. The digital Internet age opened once complex subjects to automatic reasoning. More and more subjects became part of scientific research. Take e.g. a field that was important for several thousand years for all religions and is described in detail in the Bible. We talk of strategic considerations in conflicts. In the past, the population prayed for victory in a war. Now we use technology with superior (or inferior) power. If a war is lost, we know the reasons in detail and don't earnestly think that God played a role. Of course, the pain and misery that accompanies a war is still (to a minor extent) a subject for the church although psychology and medicine solve most of the problems.

Priority for science

For centuries, Christians gave science and knowledge a clear priority over religion[6]. Modern medicine, efficient engineering, economic project

---

[6] See e.g. Hans Küng, Große Christliche Denker

management are only some example that show how industry made its way to nowadays "Industry 4.0"[7]. Logical interpretation of religious texts in the name of theology always was a central point in Christianity. Even more. Whenever a conflict arose between a religious belief and a scientific research result, the logical scientific reasoning won. Religion had to take a step back.

In the medieval ages people expected help from the clergymen when they were sick mostly with pain or malnutrition, when they were poor mostly because of too many children and bad harvests, or when they felt to be hunted by the devil. Painkiller and birth control pills changed that misery and the trust in clerics radically. Unions and democratic governments gave the poor a better perspective and a more reliable income. So, the church had to

---

[7] Industry 4.0 denotes the major steps toward the current challenge in the digital Internet age. The first industrial revolution consisted in using machinery driven water or steam power. The next step (Industry 2.0) used electricity and production lines which broke the assembly of products down in a series of specialized simple tasks. After World War II the computer started Industry 3.0. Now the full integration of the information technology systems of different companies and of different agencies has begun. The objective is described by Industry 4.0. The notation with ".0" is a play on words alluding to the practice in software technology where major releases are denoted with number before the "." And sub-releases with numbers after the first ".". This results e.g. in a software release 2.956.3.5.

step back many times. What is left for religious debate is mostly a "art for art's sake" discussion of principles without measurable value for the life of the members of the church.

Humbleness of formal science

On the other hand, Kurt Friedrich Gödel uncovered the limits of rational thinking. As a mathematics student, he worked out several theorems. To avoid deep and complicated mathematical reasoning, we note that Gödel proved that our mathematical logic is unable to understand our world completely. Having no other tool for our scientific research than pure mathematics, we must accept fragmentary understanding of our knowledge. Some say, very quick, that this is real theory. Sorry, it is not. There is one painful example namely information science. All software systems are from a scientific point of view a pure mathematical theory. Many efforts were made and are still in progress (e.g. JAVA, ECLIPSE software development tools) to create software without errors. This is not possible. Large software systems, like e.g. operating systems, hide thousands of errors. Anyway, nearly daily we get messages about faults in standards and unintended trap doors in software systems. The consequence are computer viruses, erroneous products and undocumented features. Our security problems will never stop because of Gödel's laws.

Fact is, our knowledge will increase in an even more rapid way and in parallel our humbleness is inevitable facing the things we don't know and maybe will never know. One of the open questions – once completely under the authority of religion - is about our free will. Does our body chemistry decide what we want before our brain can think and talk about our wishes?

Theologians and philosophers must learn and accept our knowledge-based world. Scientists must accept religious attitudes. And priests must accept that the Internet provides easy access to many competitional beliefs. There is e.g. one subject, the Bible does not cover at all. This is the management of political power. Suppose, you look for advice, how to negotiate conflicts with a dictator (or an erratic high-level boss). The object would be to free people, this dictator holds in his prisons, or to end a war. Jesus never acted on that level. To give the other cheek is no solution. The new testament won't give an answer. The old testament gives a rather military answer. Good advice comes e.g. from the "I Ging", a Chinese book written over centuries by emperors, high level politicians and magistrates. It takes some time to understand the logic and the text of "I Ging". Anyway, every manager and politician profits from it.

Billions of people are rich in our world. How could nowadays a priest ever describe God as a punitive God like all clerics did some hundred years ago? The concept of God as hope, joy, providing a spiritually rich life is much more adequate to our world. Theology needs interpretation of the holy texts and is used to familiarize quickly with the spirit of the time.

Improvement

One of our priests, who works in a university, came back and explained his difficulties teaching the students to trust God. They kindly discussed all subjects with him in an open attitude. But when he raised the question about trust, they were not interested and most of them simply walked away. We told him, that these students study e.g. medicine, physics, chemistry or mathematics. All these fields of science use the notion of modeling. The scientist builds models of the world with his formulas and formal concepts. All are aware that tomorrow better models will be available. Step by step, the models converge to a somewhat correct description of the world.

Scientists don't believe very much in a personal God, seen as a grandfather on a cloud, having Jesus on his right side. They think of God as the whole of the spiritual and material laws governing the many dimensions of our world. As they daily improve the models that describe this world, they naturally trust in God. This is self-evident. No need to talk about that. Our priest was astonished. This small conversation taught him a big lesson. In addition he learned about the continuing reduction of the field of theological debate in touch with reality.

Nature of Safety

All of us need an anchor in a home country. For most of us this is a town, a region, a place where people speak our own language. Today, our social network, our messenger community and our photo collection in the cloud are our home, too. At home, we feel safe. Home is a place to relax. Proportional to the growth of the digital Internet conveniences, the users, surfing in this virtual world, feel that all services and functions are happy-go-lucky.

But our virtual homes are not safe. In the U.S.A. alone, more then 3 million identities are stolen per year. Online banking, social networks, tax authorities and many more suffer from these cybercrime activities. Users alone cannot fight these criminals and they have extreme difficulties to make them stop using the user's identity in the future. A girl will be shocked to find her picture and identity in a pornographic portal in the Internet. A business man will lose customers and irritate his managers, if his identity is used in a social network with fraudulent or homosexual contents.

Technical functions cannot prevent such criminal actions. We must control our data ourselves. Rules are, never to give our personal data to everyone. Publish your posts e.g. with a pseudo name. Don't use your real address for weather services but enter the name of a nearby village. Don't post your ideas with your identity to the world instead of to your friends only. Etc. etc.

Theft of virtual identities are just one method practiced by cyber criminals. They open trap doors and invade your computer, install malfunction programs on your computer, blackmail the users by encrypting the contents of computers. Using the latest updates for the software is one action taken by a responsible user. See how much we know about our car. Why do people think that they can use a smartphone, a network connected TV and entertainment set and several computers in their house without any knowledge?

Of course, the police should hire enough personal to help citizen when they are attacked by cyber criminals. It is very expensive contracting a private support to help to recover the systems to their original state. Although we talk about high criminal energy and many cases, every day cybercrime doesn't trouble our politicians too much. But the point is that we lose a lot of productivity as more than 50% of the Internet is used for criminal and dishonorable actions.

Philosophy and religion are affected. Honest societies don't live with such high-level criminality. What is wrong in our societies? Even elections and news channels are influenced. We lie, we cheat, we humbug, we play dishonorable games, we tell only half of the truth etc. Those who do it are obviously proud of it. Some think hacking is an honorable activity. Didn't our mothers and fathers educate most of us in a Christian way? How can now so many of our offspring sin in such a spectacular way and number?

Our brain obviously confounds reality and the virtual world. There may be hundreds of studies telling us, crime videos don't harm our children. It is obvious, this is not true. Not only the children are affected. The adults dream their reality away, too. One of my friends told me that he is not interested in his income after retirement. He gave this to his wife. But his wife cannot define the terms "interest rate", "tax deduction" and "profit of a private investment". It's nice to watch television together every evening. Reality should not disturb such a happy family life. But the consequences will come to the light.

Safety and security are likewise things, we must work for. Technical protection is available, now we need mental help. Philosophy and religion should explain the basic foundations of a modern society in the digital Internet age. Personalities with the ability to distinguish between the virtual world and reality are the citizen we need today.

These personalities make our world safe. It's not technology but friendship, mutual help to control our complex digital life, and an appropriate legal framework.

Essentials of Digital Internet Age Philosophy

Modern philosophers publish interesting books on aspects of our life. None of them dares to work out a complete philosophy of the digital Internet age because of the complexity of modern times. But we don't have the choice. To plan and build our future (a family with children, a home, a job career, etc.), **we must draft a personal philosophy that supports us well in happiness and suffering**. Let's make it short.

Like all other philosophers, we cannot write a complete philosophy of modern times. But we help those who must sketch up their philosophy. Here are the highlights we value most.

- Don't expect to get a full-service philosophy from someone. **Enjoy the freedom to create your own beliefs.** Today, neither religion nor philosophy can define your objective. Antoine de St. Exupéry found that wisdom long ago.
- Ethics are an integral part of our philosophy. In contrast to religion, philosophy deduces its ethics out of philosophical considerations. Theology in our limited understanding can only reason from texts in the Bible. We suggest for your philosophy:
    - *Kant's Categorical Imperative* advises us to act always in a way that our actions could be set up as general rule. You find more about that in the Internet.
    - *Add the concept of responsibility* in a reasonable volume. (see also in the index "Bernard de Clairvaux").
    - *Human Rights Declaration* as shortly mentioned above. Wikipedia will inform you among other sources in more detail.

- **Add the ten dimensions of this book.**

Your Ten Dimensions of Philosophy and Religion

1. **"I am perfect"**: Fight AI Deformation of your Precious Personality

Our personality is challenged in the digital Internet age in many ways. But it is unique and thus precious. When we are young it starts as an option. Much depends what we make out of this gift. Here is an example. Jeweler Dentler in our city had two talents, dancing and making jewelry. He could practice both in our open society and said, this makes him feel like a king. He made a precious throne and hung it on the outside wall of his jewelry store[8]. Whenever our major gave his traditional oath declaring that he will treat rich and poor in the same way, reaching back to medieval rules, jeweler Dentler made a speech as king on his throne. Many listened to him. Now he is dead for some years. But the tradition of this throne speech is still alive. Prominent actors and writers now apply for the opportunity to participate. Another proves, we need philosophy with reasoning about our time.

---

[8] This precious throne was never stolen or damaged although attached on an outer wall accessible by everyone in the city.

Our personality is developing during our life, taking good and bad advice in its memory. The result may be a narrow-minded person full of anxiety. **If you ever investigate Artificial Neural Networks and especially the way Deep Learning works, you find the permanent print that bad training of our personality leaves in our brain.** Once damaged, there is no way back. Once we neglected our brain and our education, an integral part is damaged forever.

The same person and brain may develop to an intelligent, broad-minded, strong personality with charisma for a leadership. The latter seems to me what our children and we ourselves should become. The digital Internet age provides infinite chances for personality development. No person on our earth ever had these possibilities. Why? With the Internet we can see all important paintings, listen to all kind of good music and exchange our ideas with billions of people and organizations. There is only one thing: Do it. And do it the right way. Because good training leaves permanent prints in our brain, too.

Don't let the bad guys of the digital Internet age confuse you. They want you to lose your autonomy and to become dependent of them. This is the wrong way.

Most activities on the Internet are designed to make us dependent of something or someone. This works best if our personality is caught by one way or the other. And there are many ways. A nice app with some entertainment makes us buy our clothing or food from a specific company. Ease of use functions like "one-click-buying" make us permanent customers. We become blind to shortcomings in the company processes and routine-blinded. Totally different was shopping of our mothers and grand-mothers in their village or town. They saw new products in the shop windows on their way. They met friends, talked what they were looking for and heard new ideas and finally borrowed what they wanted to buy. Traditionally their personality grew. Blind Internet shopping based on cookies does the opposite. It blinds and reduces our personality.

We don't advocate to reduce the use of computers and digital systems. But we want to be aware of what we are doing and what is done to us. Counter-strategies are needed to make our personality grow in a good direction.

Artificial Intelligence (AI) is already everywhere in our digital knowledge-based world. When we say AI, we mean more than the correct technical definition. AI in everyday language is Artificial Neural Networks, Quantum Computers and Artificial Intelligence. Some people think, this technology is coming. This is wrong. AI technology is already implemented in many services, we daily use. Due to lack of transparency, we don't know where it is implemented. And the technology is not required to tell us how it works. There should be a law to guarantee transparency of AI applications. If the diagnosis of a disease is wrong, we are hit in our existence. If the search engine doesn't deliver the correct answer, although it could, because someone paid to have his service presented in front of all answers, we are intentionally kept stupid (deformed/distorted) and it's a burglary of our time and money. These scenarios cannot describe our future and the future of our kids.

Search engines try to give "better" service by storing and recalling our preferences. Shopping portals remember in a similar way what we were looking for in the past and what we finally bought. Electronic travel agents know what romantic or lively places we prefer and our preferred level of luxury in accommodation. The intentions of this technology are not to make us broad-minded but to make millions of people dependent of the big software and hardware providers. This only helps to make multi-billion companies even richer and more powerful.

The know-how is stored on some server of the world with the avatars[9] of Internet. AI analyzes our personality with the latest results of psychology and other science. This is not done to give us insight but to give all organizations registered with these services the opportunity to offer us services and goods we can hardly refuse. This may result in help or in pure manipulation. In both cases we should check if our personality is affected and manipulated.

Deformation of our personal development mostly reduces our motivation. The cause of deformation may be taboos or legislation like e.g. about sexual

---

[9] An avatar is a service in the digital Internet age. Usually it provides a complete service like booking a hotel or a cheap flight. If the service is satisfactory we don't know as we cannot check thousands of flights. Avatars are not yet forced by law to make their service creation transparent to the users.

orientation. When Jesus lived, probably the roman occupying forces created an atmosphere of anxiety and pressure. It was not astonishing; the Jews became sick and Jesus could free them with his charismatic (divine?) power.

In countries with liberal laws, deformation is mostly caused by self-restriction of people. Many seem to be blind to see their manifold opportunities. Instead of choosing a longer and more laborious (life-long) education, people try to make money as soon as possible. Why? They think, happiness means spending money, using digital Internet streaming services, watching many movies and knowing all stars in the fast-rotating circus of celebrities in Netflix, Spotify, Amazon etc. Such fantasies are a deformation of a personality. To become happy does not require the latest iPhone with the best camera of the universe. It rather requests that we shape our personality consistent with our natural talents and create a versatile and watchful mind.

To begin a successful way to a happy personality, we start with language. A creative and innovative personality uses an **elaborated language**. It can address people on several levels, learn new things, enter new worlds and make friends with many of the people met. An adult personality shows natural interest in other people and listens to their stories. Poetry, story books, paintings, music and architecture play an important part of the life of an educated personality. This description shows the wealth and happiness of such a personality. Success in the job is a consequence. Some decide against money-making and prefer a socially profitable way of life or other niches.

Develop our personality means to set objectives for our life. Objectives are not provided by fate or God. The chance to define our way through life, to set our personal ambitious goals, is a gift God gave us. Let's use it. Don't throw away a gift of such universal dimensions.

Choose your professional occupation carefully. I think e.g., an architect leaves a lot of buildings to remember him when he is dead. A surgeon's work is thrilling because the human body is extremely complex and medical research is incredibly successful. A lawyer's help is needed when we are in real trouble because someone attacks us heavily on legal grounds. The world is extremely rich and everyone with open eyes can find his or her happiness in it.

2. **"I find happiness and love"**: Sustainable Happiness and Love Outside the Digital World

No matter what marketing on all channels says in the Internet, **happiness** cannot be ordered or bought in a shop. Praying for happiness is by itself no success either. Register in an Internet service, e.g. a streaming service, may give some satisfaction, but it is far from happiness. The old Greek philosophers and modern ones like Kierkegaard developed their idea of happiness. One idea was to observe strictly the rules of virtue. May be this satisfied people who lived in a Greek city, which we would call a village by our modern standards. In today's world of plenty this convinces only a few.

We can get everything (knowledge with search engines, airplane tickets for some Dollars only, tickets for all museums of the world, etc.) by the fingertips. This is tempting for every intelligent being. Why not use it? But is it happiness? Probably these services are so self-evident today that happiness would be an exaggeration. For Voltaire, Goethe or Shakespeare, an airlift would have been happiness. But we comment more about the bad service than about the joy of flying.

The U.S. constitution guarantees "the pursuit of happiness". This is a good expression. It clearly says, we must work some time on it and happiness is the result. If e.g. we wish to have our own business, we work for this objective. We start small, we adapt after lessons learned and then try to grow fast. Not necessarily, we build a new company like Microsoft or Apple, but we get enough according to our abilities. The old Greek philosophers knew: "If enough is not enough for you, you can never be happy". So, the one, who builds his own enterprise, should look back happy every day. Happiness is in his work, either because he was successful or because she/he learned a new lesson. No worries, there will always be successful days, not only days with lessons learned.

The digital Internet is today a frame to become successful and happy. Using it with perfection, enables us to conquer our complex and heterogenous world. The digital Internet is a tool. Happiness is usually not found in using a tool. Whereas the designer and programmer of an Internet avatar or a digital game might be very happy.

Consuming drugs, watching TV or movie streams from the Internet does not provide any kind of sustainable pleasure. But running an Internet based business may give happiness, as the Internet provides more chances than mankind ever had. Designing your shirts, selling your photos, running a portal for people to exchange objects (clothing for kids, books, …) are all low-threshold services. According to an American study, you can make most easily a lot of money from everyday services. Offering a brand-new technology and inventing miracles are mostly condemned to bankruptcy.

Many people are happy when they learned to live without much luxury and extravagance. This takes a burden from them. In addition, it opens their eyes for the beauty and excitement near the roads they go. To walk through the outback of Australia on your own or with a good friend is happiness. Take a bike and drive through Persia. Buy a train ticket and discover India. Take your family and camp with a tent outside a park on a river. Many countries offer this opportunity. The idea is to get the maximum from investing (almost) nothing. You sure can use the experience for your job, too. All your colleagues will envy you. Enjoy this and give your acclaim to the story of your colleagues, too.

Love works different. I wrote a book in German with the title "Happiness flows to people who know to love". The point is, that love, unlike sexual attraction, needs some attention. You doubt that? We give you an example. A husband was on a longer business trip. He comes home, and the spouses ask each other to prove, that she/he still loves the other one. A trained personality knows that such questions can never be answered convincingly. Consequently, these questions should never be asked. Even asking such a question is a violation of confidence. There are many such questions in the life of a couple. May it be about sex or something like "What do you really think of my friend John / Margret / …? Tell me the full truth.". That doesn't work. The idea is that love, mostly started by some kind of sexual attraction, binds two people together. They might be loosely or tightly coupled. This is not important for the success of their partnership. The criteria for success is confidence. When they decided to live in the same household, they should develop synchronously in their common future. This is not always possible in our heterogenous world, even if both try hard. The divorce courts were invented for this desperate situation. Before going there, you should recognize that divorce often splits a rich couple in two poor singles.

The Internet offers portals to find a good partner. Income, IQs, beauty and much more are the criteria to select a spouse. From agriculture we can report, that the mating of animals is arranged according to some criteria. The European Union started that first and was successful (more meat, less bones, high quality products). Then other countries followed. But for people? Our mind is a dangerous thing. Using such portals make us dream of persons that cannot exist. Every person has drawbacks. Better learn to live with imperfect people than search for perfect partners. Obviously, our working conditions make it difficult to find a partner the traditional way. But with the ten dimensions of this book, you get a good chance.

One or two centuries ago, the members of a family lived in their neighborhood. Hardly anybody thought about a philosophy of love. They all had to stick together to survive. Today, the grand-parents have a recreational vehicle. They skype to communicate with their grand-children. Real love cannot grow at a distance and in such circumstances. Distorted personalities and painful family ties will result. One of my colleagues told me, that after many years of training and fights to get promoted, he wanted to do more with his girl of eleven in his free time. He cried, when he told me what happened. She said to him, that he was not available to her, when she was younger and would have needed him. Now, she said, she is no longer interested in him. Her statement was final.

3. **"I love heart and soul"**: Myths Create your Virtual Charisma

A **myth** is used here for a term or a notion that does not represent a clearly, scientifically defined object or term of mathematics or the natural sciences. A myth is e.g. "Health", "Sin", "Social Welfare", "America first" or "Peace". In some respect, in the digital Internet age we begin to compute myths with the help of ontologies.

If a term is not a myth, we can operate with it according to the rules of mathematical logic. As mathematical logic consists of the classical logic known already by Aristotle with "true" and "false" tables and the modern predicate logic with the "all" and "there exist" operators, it is not a very complicated thing. But, of course, the theories built on these simple concepts of formal, mathematical logic, like probability theory or Einstein's theory of relativity, are pretty complex and difficult to understand. The content of such theories are no myths.

Let us discuss, if the word "table" is a myth. Walking around my residential area, I found many different types of tables today. Most are boring garden tables with four feet and a table board on top. Then I found objects that are tables but hardly anybody might have had the idea to produce them. One was a pram, in fact a very old fashioned one, with four red feet build on top of the pram and a board nailed on these feet. It was a table with wheels and very decorative. The other was a

49

board screwed on a beam which was screwed to the wall of a house. Then we use the word table among other meanings for Excel tables and Word tables. If there is no formal definition of "table", it is a myth. But there is help. Computer Science invented a data structure called ontology that could define even so manifold objects like "table". This data structure defines in one of the common data base definition methods in detail and without exception all sorts of "tables" (defined as a group, not a special, identifiable table) that ever came across the human eye and could be imagined. A special object, that is called a table (e.g. the red table in the garden of my neighbor, called an "instance" in data base theory) is stored in the subgroup "4-feet garden table") of the meta-notion "table". Although it is a lot of tedious work, "tables" can be defined in a rather fast procedure. What is much more complicated is the definition of a language with all words and the maintenance entering new words in the data base as soon as they are found somewhere. Another myth like "cancer" can become a scientific object if it is defined in a similar way like "table" in an ontology. Large teams are required to define such notions with very broad content.

But there are myths, nobody can change, to scientific objects. Positive examples of myths are pieces of art, like music, or notions like security (if security is not defined clearly like in privacy regulations and used in this and only this meaning) or social justice. "Love", "hate", "prayer" and "God" are myths according to this definition. The reason of such a definition is that the user of myths is on erratic grounds of reasoning. Having ten persons in a group, each of them will give another meaning to any term that is a myth. One thinks, a prayer is walking in the forest and listen to the birds or climbing a scarp slope. The other is convinced that prayers are only valid if we think of God. Another is sure that prayers should come from a deep feeling of the heart, because "You can only see things well with your heart." (Antoine de Saint-Exupéry in his book "Le Petit Prince"). All are right. A discussion within the group about any one of the myths does not make sense. Another example may help: If you ever asked, why two politicians discussing e.g. social welfare will never agree, you now know the answer. **Myths have no logical value. They are neither "true" nor "false".**

Use your new knowledge of myths. First, detect the myths that other people use to direct you. Then learn to use myths to reach your objectives. Soon you'll see that the use of several independent myths increases the power of your message. Why? First, people still think that myths convey truth. We know, this is wrong. Then, people cannot analyze quickly a complex of independent myths.

A major achievement of Christianity and other world religions is the concept of **one God**. There are no more House Gods, no Bridge Gods, no River Gods etc. There is just one God. Astonishingly enough, the Christian theology communicates this one God as a three-fold God: God Father, the Holy Spirit and Jesus. During history, this theory of trinity was developed with the understanding of different power and responsibility of God, the Holy Spirit and Jesus. Most ministers now say, that trinity is just a way to communicate Christian ideas in a simple and easy to understand way. God, the Holy Spirit and Jesus are alike.

There is more like that. Most ministers preach in a double-talk way. The people listening can think of God as a person, fulfilling personal wishes, or as an abstract God representing e.g. the laws of nature. The question is of course, if these hot discussions are important in our digital Internet age. They don't help us, when we get jobless, when our identity is stolen and used by criminals in the digital Internet or when we have cancer and know, most probably we shall die within two months. Anyway, as philosophers we know: With "God" we have a myth[10] with especially broad understanding.

Most people with a scientific education have great difficulties with the concept of God as a person. Where should she/he/it be? How could she/he/it ever do what some of us pray in a rather selfish mood? God helps when we pray, the ministers say. Does God let us win in a lottery when we pray for a million Dollars? Or when we pray, the war in Syria should be over? Or when we pray that no one should suffer hunger anymore? Of course not. Praying does not mean wishing. God listens to our prayers in a very abstract way.

If God created the world, he created it with happiness und plenty of food, with violence and poverty, despair and pain. There is reason in all that (see e.g. the discussion of theodizee). Just imagine a world created by a God that is only good. A "good world" is a myth which can be defined in absurd meanings. That would e.g. be a world without different states of happiness and

[10] See our explanation of the notion myth in this book.

riches. All people would be happy in the same way. If one person gets a good job, all other persons would get the same good job. This makes us ask, how all people could ever be happy in the same way in such a superficially designed "good world". That idea of a world without pain, injuries, war etc. would not make a world. As the French say "Il faut de tout pour faire un monde."[11] The idea of a good God understood as a person is standing on weak feet as soon as you begin to analyze it with a scientifically trained brain. Such an approach would only be half of the truth. **We should train us to think of God and of the whole world in two ways: with mathematical and scientific logic and with "heart & soul".**

God confronts us with the question, what we can pray (better: meditate) for? How can we stop war? How can we feed all people on earth? How can we give education to all children? How to make our nature and environment sustainable? Etc. Etc.

The consequence is a radical increase in our responsibility. If something goes wrong or if a danger is in sight, we cannot pray in the sense of asking for a miracle that helps us. Praying means – an abstract God taken as granted – a sort of meditation and brainstorming. With these human methods, given to us by God together with our brain and a network of friends and potential friends, we must find a solution ourselves.

It is to be expected that we cannot stop all wars, all hunger and all misery even if we tried much

---

[11] You need something from everything to make a world.

more than we try these days. At least we can feel loyal to those in misery. That was an answer of Pope Franciscus when he was asked by a child, why God tolerates war and other pain. He answered, we can and must demonstrate at least our sympathy showing that we try to help.

Philosophy uses myths, too. In fact, it is needed mostly to give us orientation with the world of myths. Philosophy is built on the same erratic grounds as religion. Of course, the philosopher tries to express the basic axioms in a kind of logic and deduce his personal philosophy in a logical way.

Consequently, religion and philosophy converge in our knowledge based digital Internet world. As we did in former centuries, we simply uncover all secrets in our life. Historically it was Jesus, who taught us to do so. Manage the world, he said. Tell the truth. That's what science and philosophy is all about. As science grows, philosophy and religion shrink.

But there is still a rich world beyond science. Science is based on mathematical logic, proofs, objects of which we can prove the existence. Isn't that boring? We cannot prove the existence of beauty, love, hope, happiness, feeling safe and secure, friendship and many more non-materializable things. And we have no strictly scientific algorithms to model and calculate these things. If some of us use algorithms, these are superficial and based on primitive ideas. Some Internet portals use such algorithms e.g. to find a man or a wife to become friends and marry. We should never accept such technology as a serious part of our life.

We call this non-scientific world a world of myths. These myths, like love or social fairness, are neither logically true nor false. Myths need another way to manage them. But we must let them come into our life. Otherwise we are amputated, living mostly without a rich soul and the ability to discover love and happiness.

Managing myths is an old practice. Writers, Hollywood movie makers and many more people know for centuries how to handle myths. Myths can be seen like mathematical vectors. There are myths depending on each other, like rich, shares and market value. We can use geometric vectors to denote a myth. Interesting are myths that are orthogonal vectors. We find them in good movies or plays like the musical "My Fair Lady". There Professor Higgins makes a flower girl learn good English. The goodness of Professor Higgins, the will to learn of the flower girl and the whole setup of the play are three orthogonal myths (vectors). Together and with some minor myths added, George Bernard Shaw created a play we appreciate to see many times. We love myths and we adore a thrilling combination of orthogonal myths. Another set of orthogonal myths are e.g. in the Bible. Many stories produce real powerful imaginations. These are e.g. the virgin birth of Jesus plus the angels in the stable in Bethlehem plus the kings bringing gold. Of course, politics and commercial companies know all that. The car makers market their cars as being pure luxury, running for a million miles and providing security in all situations. These, too, are three orthogonal myths. A very simple example of orthogonal myths is the combination of "-" and ">" to an arrow "->".

Highlights of Digital Age Theology

Our jobs in the digital Internet age demand that we are always used to reason, to ask in-depth questions, to refuse information without checking its likelihood. As a customer we get easy to understand legal information, even in complex situations. We expect such service everywhere. This creates expectations. Priests should tell **with simple language** (omitting Latin, Hebrew and other confusing expert-style terms) their messages like that **there is one God**. Do not confuse people with rhetoric that does not communicate helpful information. Two examples stand for many.

- When a person dies, many parsons say "When you live, you belong to God. When you die, you belong to God. So, if you live or die, you belong to God.". This is a meaningless game of words. Remember, we believe in one God. This God must be responsible e.g. for life and death, health and sickness, happiness and desperation. The words above cannot relieve. They represent a mockery. To console someone who is going to die or who lost a near relative needs a full understanding of death. The person who dies in most cases reduced his attention to a few things still important for him, like the future of his partner and his family. The family who loses a loved person thinks how a future without the beloved (or hated) person will look like. There is much to be considered and for the parson much to say. Important is to communicate (in some, not in all situations) that death can be a relief for the family and the person who dies. If someone dies we must put him in our memory and remember what good he/she did before.

- We need a global ethic and Hans Küng provided many good ideas like we need peace and research between the religions. But the Declaration toward a Global Ethic as published by the parliament of the religions in 1993 is full of exaggerations that try to reduce our autonomy by creating fear. The introduction starts with the following words: "*The world is in agony. The agony is so pervasive and urgent that we are compelled to name its manifestations so that the depth of this pain may be made clear. Peace eludes us – the planet is being destroyed – neighbors live in fear – women and men are estranged from each other – children die! This is abhorrent.*"[12] A bad and untruthful description of our world. An ethic that makes us as individuals responsible for everything going bad in this world is no help in our daily life. If this introduction is not meant for us as individuals but for governments and parliaments, it is absurd, too. There is no army, no government and no parliament on this planet that could accept this introduction as a working program.

_____

[12] https://www.global-ethic.org/

Extend the Bible. There are so many subjects today that Jesus and the Bible never heard of and never had to deal with. Examples are gay persons, women with the full rights of men, development of technology with the potential to heal and to kill, management of a world crowded with people and suffering from climate change, negotiating with super-powers and limiting the influence of super-companies. Of course, some of the general terms of the Bible can be cited in any situation. But this would be another trivial and mocking statement. Look beyond the Bible into other books, like e.g. the I Ging. And, religious thinkers of all professions extend the Bible.

Like physics work with models, the **Christians can think of God as a person or an abstract concept**. Both models are just models, but not the truth. Do not produce rhetoric foam.

Of course, priests know how to organize a service. Sometimes they give an elaborated speech with logical reasoning. Another time they provide good music and many opportunities to sing. Then there are services for meditation based on songs from Taizé. This is good if texts apply to our modern life, don't give unrealistic hope and do not make people dream without acting for their rights and interests.

Whatever religion we are talking about, the message is to **love all other people**, especially those in need, and practice the spirit of the **ten commandments (or similar rules)** without exceptions. There are fundamentalist, aggressive and intolerant people in every religion. This is totally unacceptable as philosophy tells us, there is no truth in myths. And all religious beliefs are myths and not reality.

"Were there miracles (as reported in the Bible) or not?" is another question, which cannot be answered. Today, psychology says that Jesus' method of waking people up were mostly no miracles. Considering the stress produced by the Roman dictatorship, a well-trained psychologist with good emotional senses and charisma would help mentally sick people today with similar methods. They seem to be effective and to work very fast.

Give sense to old words. To pray means e.g. to meditate, think intensively, positively about a real problem. Eternal life means to do help many people during your life as a good example; they will not forget you.

4. **"I find friends everywhere":** Networking Makes Friends for Life

Everybody will agree that making friends is good. The social networks made a profitable business model out of that in the digital Internet age. But many don't succeed in making friends. They cannot touch the heart of their acquaintances, their neighbors and their colleagues at work. To address a sympathetic person in a shop and start small talk seems totally impossible for most people. Originally everybody wants to find new friends that way. We see this when we watch our grand-children. But if nobody teaches them to do that, they fail and from frustration tell themselves that they don't want it. Then misery begins.

When being in emotional trouble, many people look for help in a social network or a messenger service. Mails are commonly also used. Instead of inspiring new personal friends, met face to face regularly, much too many people substitute motivating personal interaction with ten-word communications with "likes" and emotional icons in digital media like social networks. This is not intended when we talk about building a personality.

There are some rules we might follow:

Remember whenever you meet someone: **You own a unique and precious personality** … if you don't hide it with distortion. You are potentially interesting to all people you meet.

John Steinbeck describes "**The Arming**" in his book Sweet Thursday. A lady in love is prepared for a meeting with her friend. How should she speak? What subjects are helpful? If her head goes to a blackout, what to do? We will not copy this funny story in our pages, but one rule is the best: **Ask questions!** This never insults anybody. With questions conversations start easily. Even when you are in a confrontation with aggressive people, asking questions to cool people down is a strong strategy.

Don't play the strong and the wisest. People dislike ("hate") superior people. Present yourself as you really are: A person not so sure of how things really work. This opens other people's hearts. They answer to you. So, if you see a nice girl in a pub, alone, then go to her and ask her, if this weather isn't making her tired, too. This is much better than telling her, that your car's engine is a plug-in hybrid. If she is interested and you are really an interesting guy (people say: "a nice guy"), both of you will wake up pretty soon anyway.

Keep your distance! Don't expect anything from the unexpected acquaintance. People are thinking about so many things and many are living in a tight time schedule. But be impressed, how many people will take the rope you are throwing and let you come near them. Keep your distance even holds, when you are married. Don't ask silly questions and don't put pressure on you partner.

Begin your answers with "Yes.". In most cases, your partner in conversations use other words than you would use, but they share your opinion. So, "yes" is always a good start for your answer. If in rare cases your partner does not share your opinion, may be even demonstrating that with hostility, begin with "yes" anyway. You stress that you have sympathy for his underlying anger. Your partner obviously feels envy and grudge. After your "yes" you cautiously address his anger. This allows you to understand him. We guarantee that you are going to know a new thrilling person, discuss important subjects and drift away from small-talk. This is the heart of networking with friends. Only if you have a gifted partner, who is eloquent in writing, you can achieve part of the conversation in written form (messenger, mail, social network). What you miss is his/her body language which reveals more than the text-content of the answer. Our brain decodes body language faster than a computer and our awareness results in the content of the answer and the body language used.

These rules are effective in face-to-face meetings and in your written communication. There are many propositions in the Internet how to write texts. The most important is often forgotten: **The text you deleted cannot be offensive or misunderstood.** Written communication often makes us blind. We overlook important side-effects like a compliment, which is expected, or by focusing on our communication partner with the question "Are you ok?". Sometimes, we think we should answer fast. Later we see, the addressee didn't read, as we expected, our answer within minutes or hours but the next day. We could have done better with more patience.

5. **"I never get tired"**: 10% for Leisure is Opening Doors for you

Everyone reading this text remembers situations when she or he were blind and didn't see the obvious. This might have been a cry for help by a stranger or a friend, an opportunity to have a charming chat with a neighbor or an interesting person we met by chance, a deviation from the road into a small way through a magnificent countryside, or something else.

May be our senior unexpectedly started talking about promotion in another city or professional field. We turned it down, because we couldn't think beyond our restrictions (consisting of our children who – we think in this moment - don't want to change school and comrades). And may be, two months later our wife asks, why Frank got the job in Philadelphia and not you? "We could have moved there easily. Our kids would have liked it."

An obstacle created by the digital Internet age is that we are always busy. Scanning our mails and messages, answering unsubstantial questions with content-less flowery phrases, looking for news we are not really interested in like sports news of a club we don't really care for, are examples. Stop that now! This is throwing away precious time, energy and self-determination.

Make it a rule for your life: 10% of your daily time is devoted to your life. During this time, you simply relax or think of your achievements and your drawbacks. You check whom you injured and whom you helped today. Think about your happiness and the happiness of the people you are fond of. Look for alternatives. Learn a bit of brainstorming[13] to get rid of your blindness. But don't overdo your help for others.

Be selfish like a good Christian mystic. Bernard de Clairvaux said about giving love to other people that the love you can spend is just like water in a bowl. If the bowl is empty, you cannot spend water. This means, if you are exhausted, sick or over-worked, you cannot spend love to other people, because you cannot even love yourself. Some Buddhistic thinkers are stricter saying, a person can help others but should never by touched by the fate of another person. Here we totally miss the aspect of responsibility and sustainable love.

To love yourself, you must investigate your heart and your soul. If you don't find love in there, you urgently must change your direction. Do mental sparring with the help of your family and your friends. Talk with them. In most cases, they will help you with good advice[14]. If they don't and they criticize or even insult you, you have got the clue. The way you are treated is the way that makes you sad. So, any way you go, you are winning. You are on your own. To make a mistake is often better

---

[13] A simple way for brainstorming is to compare your life with a Christmas tree. Where are your candles? Are there sweets hanging on the tree? What gifts would take your breath away, if you found them under the tree? What food would you like? Where would you like to have the house with the Christmas tree?

[14] To have some fun, read: Salman Rushdie, Good advice is rarer than rubies, East-West

than doing nothing. Wrong decisions can be changed.

Now, don't turn to anonymous "friends" in a social network. They most probably are of no help. First, you cannot trust them with your innermost considerations. Secondly, they may try to profit from your situation. Better check on trustworthy Internet portals for solutions. Solutions may not be one big action. Very often, the solution is to start a new way without knowing where it is finally leading to. Be suspicious and check your ideas again and again.

Many people feel **stress and fatigue** when they are in search of a new life, a new environment and may be new friends. Those who practice a balanced lifestyle with enough time for leisure feel different. These people trust their mind to find the right way. Concentration and self-absorption are the methods to become quiet and confident. This needs time, the 10% for our leisure. It needs more, we come to that in a later chapter, namely our trust in our world and in God.

6. **"I love wealth"**: Thinking without Limits Shows Ways through the Infinite Digital Internet

For centuries, everybody was convinced that we live in a **world of poverty, hardship and shortage**. But this is not true. Open your mind and search the Internet. Many thrilling and exotic occupations wait for you. As Andy Warhol said, everyone will be famous for one day in our world, there are friends waiting for you. Public interest is guaranteed in our heterogenous society always looking for the special event. Of course, as an alternative we can hide for years and come out with our products later when we feel they are fit for the public. Some artists paint only in grey and produce a new insight into our world. Some use old rags and build objects. Others produce machines with no astonishing functions out of used parts.

Our world is a world of plenty. Open your eyes and the blinds caused by prejudice. There it is, the lively, fascinating, rich and funny world. In the past, people never distributed the wealth of the world equally to all. They even invented objects that could never be distributed equally to all people like a thick jewel on a gold chain or a fortified castle on a hill. Only children know that a pebble can be as pretty as a jewel. **Based on our personal philosophy, we decide what is precious and what isn't.** It's the pebble or gold, it's the apple or the mango fruit, it's our clothing or world designer's clothing.

Who is responsible for the shortage? It's the people and the standards set by the greedy, intelligent, power-loving class. In the digital Internet age, these people come with world wide monopolies for digital systems. This reduces wealth. We should not support it.

God didn't make the world without enough food for all. On the contrary. Today, the people in the rich countries throw away so much food that the poorer ones in the third world or in the slums of the first and the second world could easily be given tasty and nutritious food in plenty.

To pray to avoid hunger is obviously not the right strategy. To fight for a just distribution of food is the right attitude. To fight cartels is another way. Of course, it's a political issue. The hungry people need jobs and an agriculture protected by fair policies. So, we must fight for the right policy.

This is one example about thinking in a creative way without accepting mental limits that were taught for centuries. More of these barriers breaking mental developments must come. Everybody must find his barriers that limit his development. We support your brainstorming with some examples. Undoubtedly, you can overcome the message sketched in these examples by yourself.

- Girls don't do that …
- If you want to make money, go into law, medical research or computer science …
- Stay in the home town where you lived as a child. There will be no protection anywhere else …

7. **"I trust my world and God"**: Increasing Uncertainty and Insecurity are no Threats

Due to the digital Internet age, smaller newspapers and other media fight to survive. The money of the marketing departments that kept these old-fashioned media alive for many years, now flows to the giant Internet companies. The directors of the smaller newspapers found only one chance to keep their readers as regular subscribers. They create anxiety by reporting about the threats and insecurity of our world. If e.g. somewhere in India a crime was done, we receive it by the media as if the crime would have been committed in our neighborhood. If a nobody talks rubbish in Europe, this is reported to the U.S.A, as if the parliament had voted on a law. So, every morning we wait for the local newspaper to arrive in our letter box with tension and even anxiety.

We could act differently. We could trust our neighbors. We could trust the medical service in our county. Usually, there is no real danger in our world. And if, with very low probability, a security issue will appear, there will be much help and support by the infrastructure, we pay our taxes for. And we could trust and elect the hard working politician instead of the one shooting out a hundred tweets per day.

We can even live without watching the evening games of politicians every night. This does not advocate that people neglect their interest in state and federal politics. But instead of being fooled by those busybody politicians tweeting daily their importance to the world, we should concentrate on those politicians who work hard for our comfort and security. These exist, too, and they need our support, even or especially when they tell us unpopular truth.

In the digital Internet age, we feel a threat from the complexity of exactly that global digital world. All of us can easily understand that. This sentence and discovery is already the solution to our insecurity. They all feel alike. Even an expert in the field of computer security, must say from time to time that an event reported was new information and must be assessed. That is a normal thing in a world with thousands of parallel events. **We have enough time to reduce complexity.** When I have trouble with my car and I don't know what's wrong, I act in the same way. I talk to friends, I look for cheap and efficient solutions and, may be, I find a neighbor who knows how to mend the broken part.

The end of the problem is that I deepened my friendship with the people I spoke to. And I got a wonderful and cheap solution. This is changing insecurity into a network of healing hands and a secure neighborhood.

As you look for good tires when the winter with snow and ice is in sight, you should protect your digital devices in the same way. The advice given below is a set of philosophical advice to be used in many more situations than just with a smartphone.

- **"Never put all your eggs in one basket!"** is a good advice for your smartphone. If it breaks or if there is a software problem in Android or another operating system or app, it is a relief to have the data on another media or on paper. Try this: First the computers were invented and now a genius comes and invents the paper. They ask him to present the advantages of the new technology "paper". Our genius says that paper does not need charging. That several people can read it from all angles. It can easily be folded. Etc. What a successful business he could start with paper!
- **Update your software if several people did so successfully before**. Of course, we can be the first and tell long and funny stories of what had happened. Once, an update locked my smartphone and I couldn't call anybody any more. But there are better possibilities to spend one's time.
- **Do only those things that you really understand**. Never just touch or brush or switch of your device if you cannot assess what's going on. You possess a precious personality. You set the standards.

8. **"I find the hidden jewels"**: Curious and Warm-hearted People are Successful

In the East, people tell the story of a princess who one afternoon enjoyed a cup of tea in her garden. When she walked up and down to watch the blossom of her trees, she saw an object falling in her cup of tea. She didn't throw it in the weeds, as many of us would have done. With natural curiosity she checked this object and discovered silk. Later, silk proved to be more precious than gold and jewels.

Silk, once discovered with the processes to weave and color it, was a task of **curiosity** and engineering. But selling it, bringing it to the markets of the world, needed other virtues. Most imported was the ability to talk, to present, to raise interest and to negotiate with people from other cultures. That's where **warm-hearted people** are coming in.

To produce a good product (e.g. in the digital world) or to formulate a true statement, many people consider the production to be most important. May be, you are not talented for production. Never mind as probably, most important is to spread the message and the product. **Engineers who invent and produce, and sales people who can sell are both very**

important! One cannot live without the other. The world needs all of us with all our talents.

We honor the people who gave us new inventions. It's a pity, we forget those who communicate and bring the inventions into the market and to their success so well merited.

The digital Internet age provides a lot of possibilities to communicate and to spread the news about new inventions. To set up an Internet portal or an information center in a social network is no big deal today. We neither need much money nor do we need to write a program. But what we need are ideas to make our communication a lighthouse in the infinite world of boring and heartless Internet portals and communication points. Success is nearly guaranteed, if we can bring our warm-hearted personality to shine through the pages of our Internet post. This creates sympathy and attracts customers.

To make friends with your natural curiosity, ask questions. We already talked about that magic attitude. When e.g. your girl-friend from school walks through the city with a pram, ask her many questions about age, behavior of her baby, her personal situation characteristics, her partner or husband. You will meet next time as very good friends. And she will ask back. So, you can carefully put your interests or even problems to her to get valuable advice. You'll soon discover that the world is small. She might name you persons to contact for a job or for selling a product or idea you found in your leisure. And then you start to organize a meeting of all your school friends.

More and more people found out that it is helpful for a business to show **an owner dedicated to an idea**. Some business people devote their time and interest to a sustainable nature. Others support and help to organize cultural events, like Jazz bands playing in the community hall. The customers of such business people can identify them. The positive impression, they get from their social actions, are transferred to their job and their business and enrich these activities.

The idea is: **Do something good and report it in the digital media.** You can e.g. attach one or two lines to your mails (in the "signature field") to inform automatically everyone who gets your mails about your positive activities.

Some people don't do as advised because they feel, they don't have the time. Their business or job or family squeezes the last resources out of them, they think. Be sure, everyone feels like that from time to time. This is normal. But it is temporary, too. Our advice is: Relax! 10% leisure and the world will not stop spinning around! Take your time to discuss it with your family, your friends or partner. Reduce the amount of work, you originally intended to attach to your social action. Start small. Tell about it anyway. Enjoy the meetings, the actions and the people you meet with your family and your friends. Many discovered this way the possibilities of help from the kids and the partner. This can bring families together. Instead of splitting in two or three groups, one having a swim and the other going to eat ice cream, suddenly the family is happy helping in the positive social event. And, maybe, there will be a photo in the local newspaper.

9. **"I show my opinion"**: "Truth, nothing but Truth" Keeps Trouble Away

"Truth, nothing but the truth!" is broader and more rigorous than the request, not to lie.

Let's first look at the subject from a personal point of view. Did you ever find someone, who could really lie? I didn't. When we started in our company with e-mails, most team-members expected to receive false e-mails. They knew, it was so easy to cheat. Why shouldn't people then do it. In fact, after more than 10.000 e-mails that our team exchanged, not a single mail was false. The reason is simple. It is very difficult to make a wrong e-mail look like a true one. You simply cannot lie so convincingly hat other people believe it. The second reason is that no one wanted to cheat.

The world is much better than we expect. And it is much more complicated to trick people than most expect.

Remember when the last time someone lied to you. Probably, you realized the lie and you knew the truth. But you didn't mention a word. That is what most people do. The person who lies gets another perspective. First, the liar cannot forget his lie. The liar must continue the game once it was started. Second, the liar drifts step by step in a world that does not exist. This makes life rather complicated. To continue a lie, even when being in a group of other people who know the truth, needs a master mind inventing more and more absurd fictional realities. Everybody knows the liar and his lies, nobody cares any more about the lies and the liar. Finally, the liar kicked himself out of his group of friends. Sooner or later, the liar needs a new group of people.

This does not look like a good perspective for someone who earnestly wants to practice philosophy and/or religion. So, let's look at the alternative.

Of course, in many situations we do not like to talk about a complicated subject or a taboo when we are suddenly addressed with a statement like "Didn't you share this opinion …..?". Then a quick lie like "No, I didn't." seems to be quite practical. But there are alternatives. We can say that the subject mentioned seems to be worth a longer discussion. Then we can continue asking for another time to speak about it. This is avoiding a lie. At the same time, we can evaluate what the people in our group were discussing and we can check our position (during the 10% leisure time). Of course, we are free to change an opinion. But all that should never be done with a lie.

Acting this way will soon make us known as a personality of high integrity. Then people say "If Joe said so, it was his opinion at the time.".

From a religious point of view, we find that the Bible prohibits to lie. It is Jesus who commands us that. Jesus never lied and thus created an impression and a charisma of an honest preacher. Could we ever imagine a religious leader who lies? No, we cannot. Jesus was always very clear and kept to the truth. In a country occupied of Roman forces that exercised force just for fun, they probably also lied a lot (e.g. when they forced a

Jew to transport their luggage for a mile), the Jews trusted only a person who undoubtedly was high above all these games. And, of course, not to lie was part of his message. Jesus wanted his miracles and messages to be told without lies, to secure his power of the holy message.

There is another aspect that has to do with the digital Internet age. At the time of Jesus, people didn't write as much as we do these days with mails, the messengers and the social networks. Information was transmitted from mouth to the ear. Then those who had received the messages travelled a longer distance. On their arrival they were expected to tell the messages in the original words again. For those who listened it was impossible to find out if the traveler lied or not. There was nobody who could have said that in the Internet another version was available. Now, we live in a different world. We can check the validity of information, especially in the western free countries, with the digital systems we can use everywhere and anytime. And today we use a rather rational language without flowery terms. We see, it is very difficult today to produce a good lie. At the time of Jesus, the situation was much different. Trust between the different villages and the people of a spiritual community like the Christians was established and maintained by a high level of truthfully told messages by all travelers.

"Truth, nothing but the truth" as a slogan for the digital Internet age requests full transparency in everything. We must know what the Artificial Intelligence software said about our x-rayed lungs. Suppose, we need an operation for our hips, we must know the ranking of the hospital for such operations. If a political party proposes a new law about private taxes, we need to know who profits and who doesn't. If in local government an organization gets permission to buy land and build apartments and houses, we request to know who profits, who is going to live there and on what conditions.

Obviously, the Bible is not rigorous enough and does not think to the end. In the digital Internet age, we know all dark methods but want to live in an honorable, free and equal society.

Our world is flooded with **fake news**, mostly because of superficial research, the lethargy to provide full transparency and the wish to produce a simple world according to our hopes amidst a complex global world. This flood of mental waste does harm our society. **The irritation produced by fake news breaks the society without any substantial reason into parts.** Where friendship once reigned, we now find reserves and injury.

Let us go back to a world where we trusted and helped each other without hesitation. Let us say the truth, nothing but the truth. We cannot convince anybody with our lies anyway.

10. **"I keep my energy"**: Fighting your Personal Way on all Channels Guarantees Strength

Dear Reader, we have gone a long way together till we arrived at this chapter. Now it's time to add up our experience. The reader should among other things now have started a network of friends, events of happiness, and love and trained his personality. Doing all this opened the mind for this last chapter. Probably, the headline is already enough for you to understand it.

It's not so easy and effortless to be always attentive and ready to act within the framework defined by our personality. Very often, we want to let us fall in this happy world of ours. Otherwise we feel tired. And especially we are not willing to fight rationally for things that momentarily – in our emotional state of love and happiness – seem to be unimportant and far away.

In such a situation, we need a balanced attitude down to the earth. To change from an emotional state to a rational discussion needs time. We must take our time. To do so, we must never forget that we have enough time. **When God created time, he or she made plenty of it.** Don't get confused by these people who always want you to hurry and to run. Life should be lived in an easy going way.

Bernard de Clairvaux was right. **If we give all our love and attention away, we don't have enough left to keep us alive in a proud philosophical or Christian way.** The temptation to act "instantly" was never so powerful than now in the digital

Internet age. But if we get a charisma of being someone who thinks before transmitting a void and meaningless message to "all", we get power and strength. They will all wait for our answer. Our answer and our attitude will set the standard in a discussion. That was exactly what we originally wanted.

They will wait. But only if we never give up. Many give up just to have a dull subject less to deal with. This is no good decision. Leave the subject open. Don't give up for peace' sake. Better you win because your adversary gives up, no matter what reason. We always presume that we fight for a just cause.

Stop before getting tired. Never let anybody exercise power on you. We do only what we are convinced that it should be done. We should never be too tired to fight.

Be positive. Especially scientists tell about people who never ever were negative. To be so perfect needs probably an education from positive parents. But we must not be perfect. Let's try: **We always use a positive, motivating way to tell our opinion.**

To do so on all channels becomes easy if we **choose one channel** that we use with the highest priority. Communication channels in this sense are talking to people, using mail or messenger or social networks. From the rule "Truth, nothing but the truth" we deduce that we must make sometimes open and clear statements. E.g., if a student asks us after two unsuccessful examinations, should he continue or not. Let's suppose, in our opinion this student is not talented enough to continue his studies, then we should say so in positive motivating words. We can mention his ability to present and to talk. We can stress that we think he could train this ability and try to get a job as a medical consultant or a computer dealer. If we write down all this, we cannot see into the face of our student and so we do not know if we should be clearer or more reserved. So, it is better not to write but to talk with him. This is one of the reasons that make me prefer as communication channel with the highest priority the traditional face-to-face communication. I saw a friend use e-mail as channel no. 1. He changed this priority when a mail he had sent was distributed in parts to many people with a wrong description of the facts underlying the mail-text. That's not possible after a nice talk. Of course, the student can report about the talk with wrong facts, but he cannot quote original text. Analogous reasons apply for mails in companies or administrations. **Whenever you write, be careful. Always describe in the first paragraph the facts as you see them. Then deduce from this description of the facts your conclusions.** This organization of your texts guarantees that you cannot be quoted in an unfair way. Never write other texts. You always have time enough to practice this rule in perfection.

May be, some guidelines to manage high workload and reduce stress can help you. Most high level managers practice these guidelines:

- Let things and processes develop, watching closely. Act only when necessary. Then make clear what you expect.

- If there is work to be done and no way to avoid it, then begin it and completer it without interruption. Many people waste their time by starting the work, doing some steps, then reconsidering it, then doing something else, then starting anew, etc. This costs precious energy and produces a negative effect on your environment.
- Don't worry about events that are more than 24 hours away. Of course, you need to plan your work for the future. If you do so, start and complete this planning task in one single step (see guideline above). Then, don't think any more about it, except if new developments occur.
- Make a list of your major worries of the last 10 years. You will see, none of these worries happened at all or in the way you worried they would happen. So educate yourself to stop worrying at all. Worries, a bad conscience etc. are useless occupations. They consume precious time and only give you a bad feeling.

Index